CHARLIE BROWN'S 'CYCLOPEDIA

Super Questions and Answers and Amazing Facts

Featuring
All Kinds of Animals
from Dinosaurs to Elephants

Volume

Based on the Charles M. Schulz Characters

Funk & Wagnalls, Inc.

Photograph and Illustration Credits: Bob and Clara Calhoun/Bruce Coleman, Inc., ix (top); K.W. Fink/Bruce Coleman, Inc., x; Copyright © 1972 by Follett Publishing Company, 100, 106, 114, 123, 140, reprinted from *Science for Human Value*; L. West/Bruce Coleman, Inc., x.

A large part of the material in this volume was previously published in *Charlie Brown's Super Book of Questions and Answers*.

Introduction

Welcome to volume 3 of *Charlie Brown's 'Cyclopedia!* Have you ever wondered why a zebra has stripes, whether owls are wise, or what "playing possum" means? Charlie Brown and the rest of the *Peanuts* gang are here to help you find the answers to these questions and many more about all kinds of animals from dinosaurs to elephants. Have fun!

Reptiles of Long Ago

What is a reptile?

The word "reptile" means that which crawls. Reptiles are animals that crawl, though some of them prefer to swim. Like fish, reptiles usually have scales on their bodies. But they breathe through lungs, as people do. They are cold-blooded animals. This means that the temperature of their blood changes when the air temperature changes. Snakes, turtles, and lizards are all reptiles. So were dinosaurs.

What are dinosaurs?

Dinosaurs were reptiles that lived a very long time ago—from about 200 million years ago to about 60 million years ago. When dinosaurs first appeared, there were not yet any birds or furry animals on earth. Dinosaurs were of many kinds and many sizes. Some had long waving necks and tails, and some had short, thick bodies. Some lived on land, and others lived in water. Some dinosaurs walked on two legs, and others walked on all four of their legs. There were dinosaurs that ate meat and dinosaurs that ate plants. Many dinosaurs had scales or a tough plate of armor on their bodies. But others had no hard covering at all.

The word "dinosaur" means terrible lizard, and scientists think that some of the dinosaurs *were* terrible and fierce. But others were quiet, peaceful creatures.

Were there people living at the same time as dinosaurs?

No. Dinosaurs died out millions of years before the first humans appeared on earth. No person has ever seen a living dinosaur. Cartoons that show cave men riding dinosaurs are just make-believe!

SAVE THE DINOSAUR

TOO LATE MARCIE. MUCH TOO LATE!

Why did dinosaurs die out?

No one is sure why dinosaurs died out — became "extinct" — but there are a few possible reasons. One is that the climate of the world changed. The warm, wet places where the dinosaurs lived became drier and cooler. The plants that some of the dinosaurs ate could not live in this new climate. When the plants died, the plant-eaters starved to death. When the plant-eating dinosaurs died, so did the meat-eating dinosaurs — since they depended on the plant-eaters for food.

Before dinosaurs became extinct, we know that new kinds of animals appeared on earth. These new animals may have caused the dinosaurs to die out. The animals may have eaten dinosaur eggs. If the eggs were all eaten, there would be no new dinosaurs. Or perhaps the new animals ate the same food as the dinosaurs, and the dinosaurs could no longer find enough to eat.

Another possible reason for the death of the dinosaurs is a world-wide disease that wiped them all out.

Scientists are not satisfied with any one of these reasons. But perhaps all these reasons together explain why dinosaurs became extinct.

How do we know what dinosaurs were like?

Today we are fairly sure what dinosaurs looked like, what they ate, how they walked, and many other things — all because we have found their bones and other remains of their bodies. These remains lay buried in the earth for millions of years and slowly turned to stone. They are called fossils. The word "fossil" means dug up.

The first dinosaur fossils were found in 1818. Many others have been found since. These fossils are mainly dinosaur eggs, bones, and teeth. Scientists can put the bones together into whole skeletons. Then they have a good idea of what dinosaurs actually looked like. By studying fossil teeth, scientists can tell whether a dinosaur ate plants or meat.

Other dinosaur fossils are footprints that have turned to stone. From these, scientists can tell how a dinosaur walked and how heavy it was.

One thing no one knows about dinosaurs is what color they were. Scientists have found prints of dinosaur skin in stone, but they are the color of the stone — not of the dinosaur.

THAT'S A DINOSAUR FOOTPRINT... YOU BLOCKHEADS!

You could easily sit in the footprint of a large dinosaur!

Which were the largest dinosaurs?

Sally is a little confused. "Bronchitis" (bron-KIE-tiss) is a disease that makes people cough. Sally probably meant to say "Brontosaurus" (bron-tuh-SORE-us) which was a very large dinosaur. But it was not the largest. As far as we know, the largest dinosaur was Diplodocus (dih-PLAHD-uh-kuss). It grew to be more than 80 feet long and maybe even as much as 100 feet long. The heaviest dinosaur was Brachiosaurus (bray-key-uh-SORE-us). It probably weighed about as much as 27 taxicabs. Brachiosaurus was so heavy that scientists believe it could hardly move on land. So it spent most of its time in water.

Dinosaur "family tree"

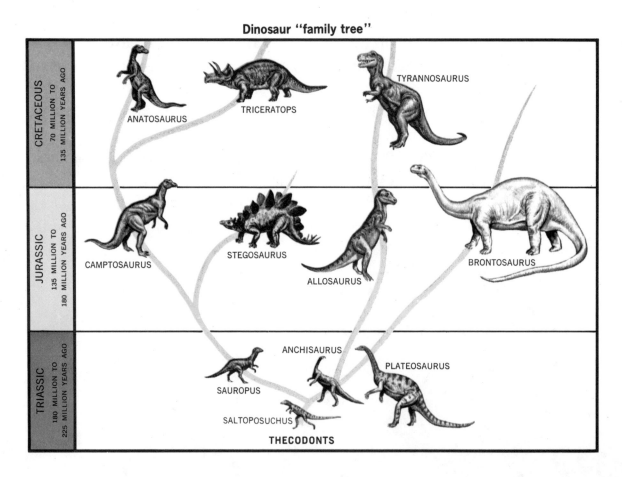

How did dinosaurs get such strange names?

The long, hard-to-pronounce names of dinosaurs all come from Greek words. Greek and Latin are the two languages the earliest scientists used. When modern scientists discover an animal or plant, they still give it a Greek or Latin name. The name is used by scientists all over the world, no matter what language they speak.

When dinosaurs were discovered, scientists gave them Greek names that described what each dinosaur was like. "Tyrannosaurus Rex" means king of the tyrant lizards. "Brontosaurus" means thundering big lizard. This dinosaur was so big that the ground probably shook like thunder when it walked. Stegosaurus (steg-uh-SORE-us) was covered with hard, bony plates and spines. Its name means cover lizard.

Were there any flying dinosaurs?

No. There were no flying dinosaurs, but there were some flying reptiles called Pterodactyls (ter-oh-DACK-tilz). None of these reptiles actually flapped their wings and flew. Instead they all glided through the air — sailed along on the wind. Their wings were made of tough skin stretched between the long front legs and short back legs.

What other reptiles lived in the days of the dinosaurs?

Quite a few water reptiles were around then. One of these was Elasmosaurus (ee-laz-muh-SORE-us). It was probably the closest thing to a sea monster that anyone could imagine. It had a very long neck, and strong legs like flippers for swimming through the water.

Tylosaurus (tie-luh-SORE-us) was a sea reptile that looked something like a modern crocodile. It was a fierce animal with large jaws and very sharp teeth.

Archelon (AR-kuh-lon) was a giant water turtle. The biggest ones weighed 6,000 pounds each and were as long as a large car. Archelon looked very much like any turtle you might see today — except it was much bigger.

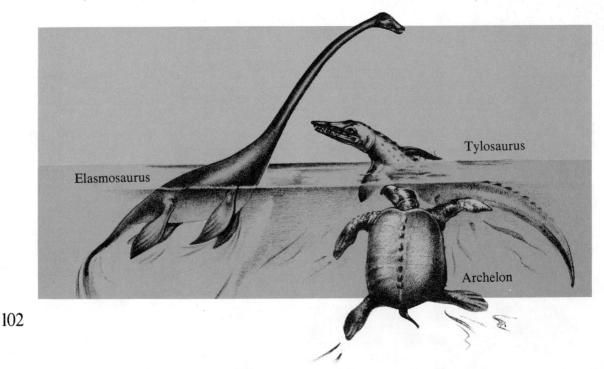

Elasmosaurus

Tylosaurus

Archelon

Reptiles of Today

What kinds of reptiles are living today?

Today there are five kinds of reptiles. These are snakes, lizards, turtles, crocodiles and their relatives, and the tuatara (too-uh-TAH-ruh).

What is the tuatara?

The tuatara is a reptile left over from the days of the dinosaurs. All its closest relatives died a very long time ago. But the tuatara somehow survived in one part of the world — on islands near New Zealand.

The tuatara looks like an odd, big-headed lizard. It does everything slowly. It breathes only once an hour. Its eggs take more than a year to hatch, and a baby takes 20 years to grow up.

Why do reptiles stay underground in winter?

Because reptiles are cold-blooded animals, the temperature of their blood changes with the weather. When the air is warm, their blood is warm, too. When the weather gets cold, the temperature of their blood goes down. The reptiles can get too cold to stay alive. So, to keep from dying, they find a protected place in which to spend the cold days. They may stay in underground holes, in caves, or under rotting tree stumps. Even in these protected places, the reptiles are too cold to move. They lie still until the air warms up. Then they come outside again. Of course, when reptiles live in places that stay warm all year long, they never have to go underground — except to hide.

Which is the biggest reptile living today?

The biggest reptile is the salt-water crocodile. This animal is usually about 13 feet long and weighs about 1,000 pounds. But it sometimes grows even larger.

I WANT MY MOMMY!

WARNING!
HUNGRY CROCODILES
PLEASE
WATCH YOUR DOG.

What is the difference between an alligator and a crocodile?

The easiest way to tell the difference between an alligator and a crocodile is to look at their faces. The crocodile's face is long and pointy. The alligator has a shorter, wider face. When the crocodile's mouth is closed, its teeth still show. But the alligator does not show any teeth when its mouth is closed.

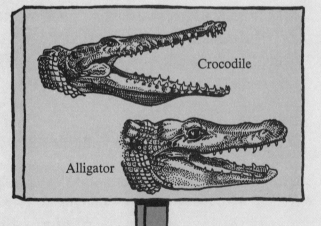

Crocodile

Alligator

Do men really wrestle with alligators?

Yes, they do. You can see these wrestling matches in Florida. Such a match looks very dangerous for the man, but it isn't as dangerous as it seems. An alligator can't bite when its mouth is held shut. So the man just holds the alligator's jaws shut while he wrestles with the animal.

Do alligators and crocodiles eat people?

Yes, some of them do eat people. Almost any hungry crocodile or alligator may attack a person who comes close to it. But the African crocodile (found only in Africa) and the salt-water crocodile (found from Southeast Asia to Australia) are the real man-eaters. Hundreds of people are killed by these animals every year. American alligators and crocodiles usually leave people alone.

I CAN'T BELIEVE IT!

SNIF

How slimy are snakes?

Snakes are not at all slimy. In fact, their skins are quite dry, and they feel something like leather. But people may think a snake is slimy when they see one sitting in the sun. When the sun shines on a snake, its skin looks shiny and almost wet.

I AGREE. YOU DO HAVE NICE TEXTURE...HOWEVER, I PREFER MY BLANKET.

BLEAH!

Why do snakes always stick out their tongues?

Snakes stick out their tongues in order to pick up smells and to feel things. Although many people think a snake's tongue is a stinger, it is perfectly harmless. The snake is simply touching and smelling with it.

105

Why do snakes shed their skins?

As a snake grows, its skin gets too small and tight for it, just as your shoes get too tight when your feet have grown. So the snake grows a new skin and gets rid of — or sheds — the old one. The snake may do this three or four times a year. Because young snakes grow faster than older snakes, the young ones shed their skins more often.

Timber rattlesnake shedding skin

Are snakes useful to us in any way?

Yes. Snakes eat rats, mice, and harmful insects — pests that eat millions of dollars' worth of crops each year and also spread disease. Snakes also eat some animals that are helpful to man, such as insect-eating frogs and birds. But, at least as far as people are concerned, snakes do more good than harm.

How can a thin snake swallow a fat rat?

An amazing thing about snakes is that they swallow their meals whole. Large snakes can swallow whole rats and whole pigs, and sometimes even whole goats!

A snake's jawbones are attached very loosely so that its mouth can stretch very wide. The snake can swallow an animal that is even bigger than its own head. The rest of its body can stretch, too, so the meal can fit inside.

106

A snake swallowing a bird's egg

Do snakes ever eat people?

Although most snakes eat only insects, mice, and other small animals, two kinds of snakes do occasionally feast on a human being. Pythons (which can be found only in Asia and Africa) and anacondas (which can be found only in South America) are the two man-eaters. None of the snakes that live in the United States are big enough to eat people.

GOOD GRIEF. I'M GLAD I LIVE IN THE GOOD OLD U.S.A!

Which is the longest snake?

Some anacondas grow to be more than 20 feet long. The biggest one ever measured was 37½ feet. That's about as long as seven bicycles lined up in a row.

Are fangs teeth?

Yes, a snake's fangs are a special kind of teeth. All snakes have teeth, but only poisonous snakes have fangs. Fangs are hollow teeth with a tiny hole at the bottom. When a fanged snake bites an animal, a poison called venom is forced through the fangs into the victim. A poisonous snake bites small animals in order to kill them for food. A snake bites people and other large animals only if it is scared and wants to protect itself.

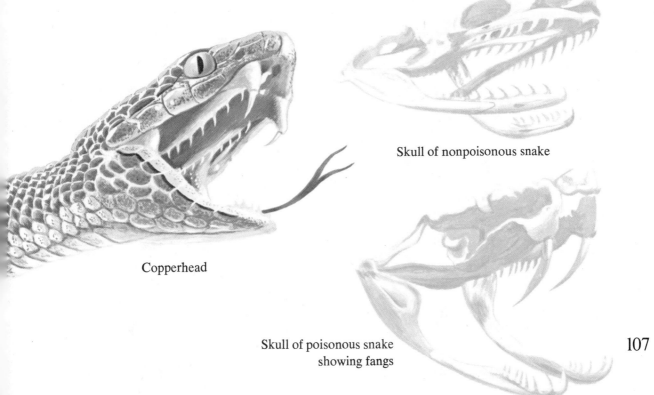

Skull of nonpoisonous snake

Copperhead

Skull of poisonous snake showing fangs

107

How many snakes are poisonous?

Actually, only 200 of the 2,400 known kinds of snakes are poisonous.

Do any poisonous snakes live in the United States?

Yes, four kinds of poisonous snakes live in the United States. These are the rattlesnake, the copperhead, the water moccasin, and the coral snake. Of these four, the coral snake has the strongest venom. Fortunately, the coral snake is small and scarcely ever bites anyone. The other three kinds of poisonous snakes have venom that takes a long time to kill a person. The victim has time to go to a doctor and get an anti-venom shot.

Sonora Mountain king snakes look almost exactly like poisonous coral snakes. But they are so friendly and harmless that people keep them as pets!

Coral Snake

How do rattlesnakes rattle?

At the end of a rattlesnake's tail are a few hard rings, made of a material something like your fingernails. When the rattlesnake is excited, it usually shakes its tail. The hard rings hit against each other, making a rattling noise.

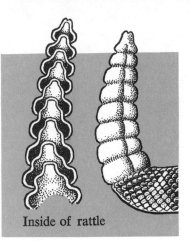

Inside of rattle

Can snakes be charmed?

No. In India, men called snake charmers play music for cobra snakes, and the cobras seem to dance to it. But they are not really dancing. The snakes cannot even hear the music—they are completely deaf! But the snakes can feel vibrations in the ground. A snake charmer taps his foot as he plays and sways in time to the music. A cobra feels the tapping, gets excited, and rears up ready to strike him. When a cobra is ready to strike, it watches its victim carefully and follows the victim's movements. And that's just what a cobra does with a snake charmer.

The snake charmer is taking a big chance when he excites a cobra. Cobras have a deadly venom and strike at people often. But somehow the snake charmer knows how to keep an excited cobra from actually striking. He really must know his business! Some snake charmers remove the cobras' fangs to be on the safe side.

109

The matamata turtle has wormy-looking bumps on its neck that fish try to eat. But instead, the matamata eats the fish!

How long can a turtle live?

No one is sure how long turtles live, but some can probably live for a very long time—100 or maybe even 150 years.

Spotted turtle

Can you tell the age of a turtle by its shell?

By looking at its shell, you can tell the age of a young turtle, but not of an old turtle. The top of a turtle's shell is divided into sections. These are called shields. On each shield are little circles. In a young turtle, each circle stands for a year's growth. For example, a two-year-old turtle has two circles on each shield. After five or ten years, however, you can no longer find out the turtle's age by the circles. They have either become too crowded together or have begun to wear off.

Wood-turtle shell showing shields

Can a turtle crawl out of its shell?

No, a turtle cannot crawl out of its shell. The shell is attached to some of the turtle's bones.

110

Common pond turtle

Where do turtles live?

Some turtles live in rivers, lakes, or ponds but often come out on land. These are sometimes called terrapins. Other turtles—ones with flippers—spend most of their life swimming in the ocean. There are also large turtles that always live on land. These have fat legs that look somewhat like an elephant's. People sometimes call these turtles tortoises (TORE-tus-uz).

Which is the largest turtle?

The largest turtle is the leatherback. It is a sea turtle that usually weighs between 600 and 800 pounds. The biggest one ever caught weighed nearly 2,000 pounds and was almost eight feet long.

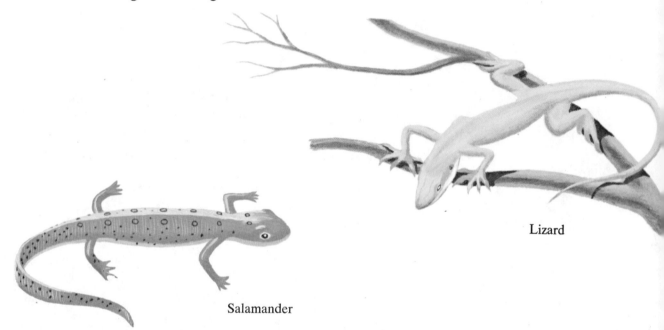

Lizard

Salamander

What is the difference between a lizard and a salamander?

Some lizards look very much like salamanders. However, the two animals are quite different. Salamanders are amphibians. Most amphibians begin their life in water, breathing through gills like fish. Only after they have grown up are they able to live on land. Lizards, which are reptiles, are born with lungs. They always live on land.

Lizards have scales covering their bodies. Salamanders have smooth, moist skins without scales. Lizards love the sun, while salamanders stay away from it.

111

Can lizards grow new tails?

Some lizards can. The gecko, the glass snake, and the skink are three of the lizards that grow new tails. If an enemy catches one of them by the tail, the lizard can drop the tail and run away. The lizard then grows a new tail. If only a piece of its tail is broken off, the lizard will sometimes grow back the missing piece and grow a whole new tail as well. So if you ever see a lizard with two tails, you'll know how it got them.

Are any lizards poisonous?

Only two out of about 3,000 known kinds of lizards are poisonous. One of these is the Mexican beaded lizard. The other is its cousin, the Gila (HEE-luh) monster. The Gila monster lives in Mexico and in the southwestern United States. People can die from the bites of these two lizards, but seldom do. The lizards don't usually put enough poison into people to kill them.

Can lizards change their color?

Some lizards can. These include the anole, sometimes called the American chameleon (kuh-MEE-lee-un), and the true chameleons. They can turn different shades of brown and green. Their color depends on the amount of light hitting them, the temperature of the air, and whether they are calm or scared.

A chameleon often turns the same color as its background. A chameleon on a log may be brown, and one on leaves may be green. Enemies have a hard time spotting it. And if a chameleon is partly in the sun and partly in the shade, an enemy can get really confused—because the chameleon will be two different colors at once!

Is the horned toad a reptile?

Yes. In spite of its name, the horned toad is not a toad at all. It is a kind of lizard that lives in the desert.

Horned toad

! A scared horned toad will squirt blood from its eyes! !

Do dragons really exist?

Dragons like the ones in storybooks do not exist. Long ago, people believed that there were great winged reptiles that breathed out fire. People in Europe believed that these dragons were evil. The Chinese, on the other hand, believed that these dragons were gods.

Today there do exist huge reptiles called Komodo dragons. They are the largest lizards alive. These dragons can grow to be ten feet long and weigh 300 pounds. They look like storybook dragons without wings. But they do not breathe fire, and they are not evil. Neither are they gods. They are simply huge animals that get hungry and have to eat. Any living creature around a hungry Komodo dragon had better watch out!

Birds

What was the world's very first bird?

The first bird was Archaeopteryx (ar-kee-OP-ter-ix). It lived about 140 million years ago. This bird was very much like a reptile. In fact, its ancestors *were* reptiles. Like a reptile, Archaeopteryx had teeth and a long, bony tail. But Archaeopteryx had feathers instead of scales. For this reason scientists call it a bird. The wings of Archaeopteryx were like a modern bird's wings—with bones inside and feathers outside. But Archaeopteryx was not able to fly well. It couldn't flap its wings very hard. It probably used them more for gliding—sailing through the air.

Archaeopteryx

I HEAR WINGS...

What is a bird?

Any animal that has feathers is a bird. All birds have two wings and two legs. Except for bats, they are the only living animals with bones that can fly. Modern birds have no teeth. But they have a hard mouth part, called a bill or beak, which helps them catch and eat their food. All female birds lay eggs, and most birds build nests for the eggs to hatch in. Birds—like people—are "warmblooded." Their body temperature stays about the same no matter how hot or cold the air is.

Hummingbird

How many different birds are there?

About 9,000 kinds of birds live on the earth today. Birds can be found almost everywhere except the North and South poles.

Why do birds have feathers?

Feathers help a bird to keep warm. In cold weather, a bird fluffs up its feathers and traps a layer of warm air under them. The fluffed feathers act as a blanket by holding in body heat. In warmer weather a bird squeezes its feathers against its body to let body heat escape.

Feathers also help a bird to fly. In flight, a bird uses its outer wing feathers to move forward in the air. Wing feathers and tail feathers are both used for balancing, steering, and braking.

Why do some male birds have brighter colors than females?

Bright colors help a male bird to attract a mate. His colors are brightest during the mating season. He flies or parades in front of a female, showing off his pretty feathers. He may also sing or dance to get her attention.

Scarlet tanagers

How do birds learn to build nests?

Birds don't learn to build nests. Nest-building is an instinct. Each kind of bird is born knowing how to build its own kind of nest. Many birds make a cup-shaped nest out of twigs and grass. Cardinals and thrushes make this kind of nest. Some swallows make their nests out of mud balls, which they attach to cliffs or the eaves of buildings. Some birds, such as titmice, make their nests in a hole in a tree or rock. They line the bottom of the hole with grass, feathers, fur, and moss. Certain weaverbirds make complicated "apartment-house" nests out of stems. These nests may be ten feet high and hold 100 or more birds.

Swainson's thrushes

Cliff swallow

Do all bird eggs look like chicken eggs?

Most eggs are shaped the same as chicken eggs, but they have different sizes and colors. Large birds lay large eggs, and small birds lay small eggs. The colors of eggs vary from one kind of bird to another. The eggs often blend in with the colors around the nest so an enemy can't spot them easily. Eggs may be light blue, brown, white, gray, or green. A few are red or pinkish orange. Some eggs are spotted or speckled.

OSTRICH EGG

CHICKEN EGG

MALLARD EGG

CROW EGG

ROBIN EGG

HUMMINGBIRD EGG

Which bird lays the smallest egg?

A hummingbird—which is the smallest bird—lays the smallest egg. Its egg is only about half an inch long.

Which bird lays the biggest egg?

The ostrich—which is the biggest bird—lays the biggest egg. This egg can be as long as eight inches and can weigh up to four pounds.
If a 250-pound animal sat down on an ostrich egg, the egg would not break!

117

Why do birds sit on their eggs?

Birds sit on their eggs to keep them warm. When an egg is kept warm, the baby bird inside can grow.

Do all birds eat worms?

No. Different kinds of birds eat different kinds of food. Usually birds have favorite foods, but will eat some other things, too. Many birds like worms and insects best. Birds that live near water often eat fish or shellfish. Owls, hawks, and eagles eat meat — mice, rabbits, smaller birds, snakes, and other animals. Many small birds, such as sparrows, live on seeds. Some birds eat mostly fruit and berries. Hummingbirds like to drink the sweet liquid called nectar that is found in flowers.

Why do woodpeckers peck at trees?

Woodpeckers peck at trees to get food. They eat insects that live in the trees, just under the bark. Most woodpeckers also peck out nesting holes in trees.

Great black-backed gull

Herring gull

Why can birds fly?

A bird's body is specially built for flying. It is very light. There are pockets of air in it, and most of the bones are hollow. So a bird doesn't have to lift much weight into the air. A bird has very strong muscles for flapping its wings. And the wings have just the right shape for flying. The inner part of a bird's wing is like the wing of an airplane. It lifts the bird up in the air. The outer part of the wing acts as a propeller. Its long feathers pull on the air and move the bird forward.

Some birds will fly upside down to attract a mate!

Can all birds fly?

No, a few birds cannot fly, but most of them are very fast runners or swimmers. The ostrich, the cassowary (KASS-uh-wer-ee), the rhea (REE-uh), the emu (EE-myu), and the kiwi (KEE-wee) are all non-fliers. They have wings, but their flying muscles are not strong enough to be useful. Penguins also can't fly. They have wings like flippers, which they use to swim and dive power-fully. Chickens cannot fly very well, but they can flutter around a bit.

Adelie penguin

Streamertail Hummingbird

Blue Throated
Hummingbird

Ruby Topaz
Hummingbird

How can a hummingbird stand still in the air?

A hummingbird can stand still, or "hover," in the air because it can beat its wings very fast—from 55 to 90 times in one second! Its wings move so fast that they look like a blur. A hummingbird hovers in front of flowers when it drinks nectar from them.

Why do birds sing?

Bird songs are not just pretty music. Birds usually sing to tell other birds of their kind to keep away from their nesting area. Often birds sing to attract a mate. And sometimes they seem to sing just for the fun of it.

Nightingale

Do all birds sing?

No. Female birds rarely sing, and only about half the males have songs. But nearly all birds give calls. Calls are short, simple sounds. The "whoo-whoo" of an owl is a call. So is the "cluck-cluck" of a hen.

Calls are often used to express alarm and warn other birds of danger. Birds "talk" to their babies with calls. Baby birds use calls to say they are hungry. Non-singing males have special calls that take the place of songs.

A small number of adult birds make no sounds at all. But these birds do make a lot of noise when they are young.

Where do birds go in the winter?

Before winter comes, many birds that live in the north fly south where the weather is warmer. In the spring, they fly north again. We say that those birds "migrate." No one is sure why birds began migrating, but the need for food was probably the main reason. In cold places there are few insects, flowers, fruits, and seeds around for birds to eat. Ponds and streams are frozen over, so fishing birds cannot get food either. In warm places, food of all kinds is available.

Every year Arctic terns fly 11,000 miles south to Antarctica and 11,000 miles back home again. They fly 22,000 miles each year!

BIRDS OF A FEATHER
AY MIGRATE TOGETHER
BUT NOT WOODSTOCK.
E GETS TOO HOMESICK.

How do birds know when to fly south?

No one is sure of the exact answer to this question. We do know that in the fall the weather gets cooler, and the days get shorter. Somehow these changes affect a bird's body so that the bird knows it's time to migrate. Scientists are still trying to find out exactly what happens inside birds at migration time.

Does an ostrich really stick its head in the sand to hide from an enemy?

No, an ostrich isn't that stupid. What this tall bird does is fall down flat when it sees danger in the distance. An enemy may not spot the ostrich in this position, or it may think the ostrich is just a bush. As soon as danger comes near, however, the ostrich will take off and run. Although an ostrich cannot fly, it can run as fast as 40 miles an hour.

Are owls really wise?

Owls are no wiser than many other birds. In fact, some birds are smarter. But owls have large staring eyes, which make them look as if they are thinking very hard. That's probably why people started calling them wise.

An owl turns its whole head upside down in order to see above it!

Which is the most dangerous bird?

The cassowary is the most dangerous bird in the world. It has a sharp claw on each foot and can kick very, very hard. One kick can cripple or kill a grown person.

Brown creeper

How do birds protect themselves?

Birds protect themselves by always listening and watching for danger. At the smallest sign of it, they will fly away. That's why it is almost impossible to get very close to a wild bird. Birds that cannot fly are often able to swim fast, or run quickly and kick, too. Some birds—such as owls—make themselves look bigger and more dangerous by fluffing out their feathers. Other birds will hiss at enemies and scare them away.

Another important protection for many birds is their color. Their feathers often have colors and patterns that match the things around their nest. Some birds are streaked with colors that imitate leaves, bark, or grass. Some birds, such as the ptarmigan (TAR-muh-gun), change colors with the seasons. In the winter the ptarmigan is white to match the snow. In the summer it is mostly brown to match the ground.

Why have some birds become extinct?

Some kinds of birds have become extinct because people have killed all of them. In the past, hunters killed birds for their colored feathers, their oil, or their meat. Today some farmers are killing large birds that sometimes eat small farm animals. Certain eagles and hawks may become extinct for this reason.

People also kill birds without meaning to. When people cut down forests and fill in swamps to build houses and factories, they destroy the homes and the food of birds. If the birds have nowhere else to go and nothing to eat, they die out.

Pollution may soon cause some birds to become extinct. Birds that eat fish from polluted water get poison in their bodies. Then they can't lay healthy eggs. New birds aren't born.

The dodo, the passenger pigeon, the great auk, and the Carolina parakeet are some of the birds that have become extinct. Other birds have nearly died out. But they have been saved because people who care have protected them.

Americans have shot and killed hundreds of thousands of bald eagles. Yet the bald eagle is our national bird!

How do people protect birds?

People protect birds by passing laws to control hunting and pollution, by setting up special parks called bird sanctuaries (SANK-choo-er-eez) where all birds are safe from hunters, and by teaching other people to care about birds rather than kill them.

Mammals of Long Ago

What are mammals?

Mammals are animals that drink milk from their mother's body when they are babies. No other animals do this. Most baby mammals grow inside their mother's belly before they are born. Most other animals grow inside eggs that their mother lays.

All mammals are warm-blooded. This means that their body temperature always stays about the same. And they are the only animals that have hair or fur. (Some insects are fuzzy, but they don't have real hair.) Most mammals have four legs, or two arms and two legs.

Dogs are mammals. So are cats, giraffes, bats, cows, horses, rats, monkeys, and dolphins. And you are a mammal, too.

When did the first mammals appear?

The first mammals appeared about 180 million years ago. They probably looked a lot like shrews or rats, having long, pointed snouts and long tails. There were few kinds of mammals on earth at first, but there were great numbers of dinosaurs. As many of the huge reptiles began to die out, mammals became the most common land animals. This change began about 65 million years ago. At that time, many new kinds of mammals appeared on earth.

What were some of these new kinds of mammals?

The ancestor of the horse—the eohippus (ee-o-HIP-us)—was one. This animal was about the size of a small dog. It had three toes on each hind foot and four toes on each front foot. Over millions of years, the horse grew bigger and bigger, until it got to be the size it is now. And over the years it lost some toes, and so now it has only one on each foot.

Eohippus

About 25 million years ago, the first doglike and catlike animals appeared. Some of the cats developed into large, fierce animals. One was the saber-toothed tiger. It was about the size of a modern tiger, but two of its front teeth were very long—about eight inches!—and very sharp. Even the largest animals were probably scared of it.

One of these large animals was the rhinoceros. It too started out small. But as millions of years passed, it became larger and larger. Huge groups of rhinos moved north to cold lands and grew thick coats of hair. These rhinos were called the "woolly" rhinos.

Saber-toothed tiger

There were also woolly mammoths. These appeared about two million years ago and became extinct only about ten thousand years ago. Mammoths were related to elephants. They were very large and had long, thick hair. Scientists know exactly how they looked, because whole mammoths have been found frozen in ice.

Millions of years ago there were also many odd-looking beasts. They lived for hundreds of thousands of years and then died out. One was Glyptodont (GLIP-toe-dahnt). It was very much like a modern armadillo, but a lot larger. Glyptodont was about 15 feet long and had a tough shell around its body—much like a turtle's. At the end of its tail were spikes. Glyptodont probably used its tail as a club and swung it at enemies.

Woolly mammoth

Ancient Glyptodont

127

! The dog family has been on earth for about 15 million years! **!**

How do we know about early mammals?

We know about them because people have found stone fossils of their bones and teeth in the earth. And people have found real bones and teeth in large pits of tar in La Brea, California. About one million years ago, thousands of animals sank into these tar pits and died. The tar hardened and kept their bones almost perfectly. The bones were very easy to dig out and to study. Saber-toothed tigers, mammoths, vultures, snakes, camels, and ground sloths were some of the animals found in the La Brea tar pits.

Many mammals have also been found frozen in the ice in the far north. Just the way a freezer keeps food from spoiling, the frozen ice kept whole animals from rotting away for hundreds of thousands of years. Many woolly mammoths and woolly rhinos have been found in ice.

An excellent record of animals that lived about 35,000 years ago was left by early people. These people lived in caves and painted pictures of animals on the cave walls.

Which was the biggest land mammal ever to live?

The beast of Baluchistan (buh-loo-chih-STAN). This huge animal looked something like an overgrown rhinoceros. It died out about 20 million years ago. The beast could grow as large as 37 feet long and 25 feet tall. It weighed as much as 22 tons. One of its legs alone was much larger than a grown man!

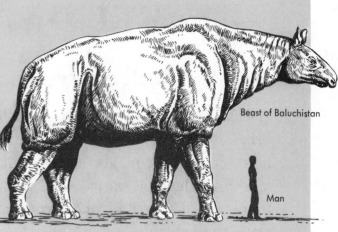

Beast of Baluchistan

Man

When did people appear on earth?

According to scientists, the first real people appeared on earth about two and a half million years ago.

What did the first people look like?

Scientists think they probably had thick hairy bodies, no chins, short necks, and long arms. Enough bones have been found to make us believe that these people stood about five feet tall. But they did not stand completely straight. Instead, they walked with their heads bent forward. These people had bigger brains than other animals, and they were smarter. They made the first stone tools and figured out how to build a fire.

KIND OF SHAKES YOU UP, DOESN'T IT?

SIR?

Dinosaurs were on earth about 140 million years. People have been on earth only about 2½ million years!

Mammals of Today

Why is a whale called a mammal?

A whale lives in water, and has a fishlike shape and no legs. But a whale is not a fish. It is a mammal, and it acts like one. A whale—like other mammals—grows inside its mother, is born alive, drinks milk from its mother's body, breathes air through lungs, is warm-blooded, and has some hair but no scales. A fish, on the other hand, usually hatches from an egg, does not drink milk, breathes underwater through gills, is cold-blooded, and usually has scales.

LAUGH IF YOU WISH, MY FINE-FINNED-FRIENDS, IT'S CALLED A DOG PADDLE.

Is there any mammal that doesn't grow hair?

No. Every mammal has some hair at some time in its life. The dolphin, a relative of the whale, has no hair when it is grown up. But it is born with a few bristles of hair around its snout. The armadillo has a scaly shell like some reptiles. But it also has hair on the underside of its body. The pangolin (pang-GO-lin) is covered with scales, but they are made of hairs that are stuck together. Porcupines and hedgehogs have sharp "needles" coming out of their bodies. These needles are really a special kind of hair called quills.

Can porcupines shoot their quills?

No, they can't. But their quills are sometimes found stuck in other animals. That's probably how the "shooting" story got started. Actually, porcupine quills get stuck in an animal when the porcupine touches it. The quills come off the porcupine very easily. Its tail is particularly full of loose quills. When another animal attacks, the porcupine swings its tail at the enemy. Quills are driven deep into the enemy's flesh. The enemy runs off in pain. Animals that attack porcupines learn their lesson quickly and don't bother them again.

Why do beavers build dams?

Beavers build dams in the shallow water of streams in order to make the water deeper. A beaver dam is a wall that keeps water from flowing past it. The water builds up behind the dam and gets deep. The beavers then build their home in the deep water, where enemies can't easily reach them.

How do beavers build dams?

Beavers have four very sharp front teeth. With these teeth, they cut down trees and then cut the trees into pieces. The cut logs and branches are used to make their dams.

A family of beavers usually work together to build a dam. They make a base of logs across a narrow part of a stream. They weigh it down with rocks and mud. On top of this heap, they pile more and more logs and branches. They fill in the holes with mud, which they carry to the dam in their front paws as they swim through the water. A finished dam is a wall about three or four feet high.

Beaver

One group of beavers built a dam more than 2,000 feet long.
That's longer than the Brooklyn Bridge in New York City!

Can groundhogs predict weather?

No, they can't. Groundhogs, also known as woodchucks,
hibernate all winter in a hole in the ground. The story goes
that on February 2—Groundhog Day—the groundhog comes
up out of its hole. If the day is cloudy and the groundhog can't
see its shadow, the cold days of winter are over. If the groundhog sees its shadow, the animal returns to its hole. Then we are
supposed to have six more weeks of cold weather.

This story is fun, but there is no truth to it. Groundhogs
stay in their holes until the weather warms up enough for them
to come out. This may happen much later than February 2, or
even earlier. Once outside, groundhogs don't look for shadows.
They just go about their business—which is *not* predicting the
weather!

FEB
2

What does "playing possum" mean?

Charlie Brown knows what he's talking about. The expression "playing possum" comes from a habit of an animal called the possum, or opossum. It falls over limp, as if it were dead, whenever danger is near. This act protects the opossum. Most meat-eating animals like to kill their own meals. They are not interested in an animal that lies still and already seems to be dead.

People used to think that the opossum purposely played a trick on its enemies by pretending to be dead. But now we know that the possum passes out when danger is near. It is not playing at all.

Why do skunks give off a bad smell?

Skunks give off a bad smell to protect themselves from enemies. When a skunk is angry or frightened, it shoots an oily spray into the air. This bad-smelling spray comes from two openings near the skunk's tail. If the spray hits the face of an animal, it burns and stings. It also tastes terrible. But the smell alone is enough to chase away any enemy.

When the spotted skunk gets ready to spray, it stands on its front legs with its back ones in the air!

Do cats really have nine lives?

No, cats don't have nine lives. But they seem to because they often live through dangers that might kill another kind of animal. For example, cats can walk on a very narrow ledge without falling off. They have a very good sense of balance. If they do fall or jump from a fairly high place, they almost always land on their feet — lightly and unharmed. Cats can also escape easily from an enemy because they can move quickly.

SO YOU FINALLY DID IT. YOU GOT INTO A FIGHT WITH THE CAT NEXT DOOR.

IT WAS A MASSACRE. NINE LIVES AGAINST ONE!

Why do a cat's eyes shine at night?

A cat's eyes shine because they reflect light. Even in the darkest night, there is usually some stray light from a street lamp or the headlights of a car. A cat's eyes reflect this light because they have a special coating on them. The coating helps the cat see in the dark, and also makes the cat's eyes shine.

House cats are not the only cats with eyes that reflect light. Jaguars, lions, tigers, cougars, leopards, and all other cats have eyes that shine at night.

What is the world's fastest mammal?

The fastest mammal is a wild cat called the cheetah. It can run at more than 60 miles an hour, and sometimes as fast as 70 miles an hour. But the cheetah can keep up this speed for only a short distance. Then it slows down.

SPEED LIMIT 55

WILD CATS! I HOPE THEY GET A TICKET

Cheetahs

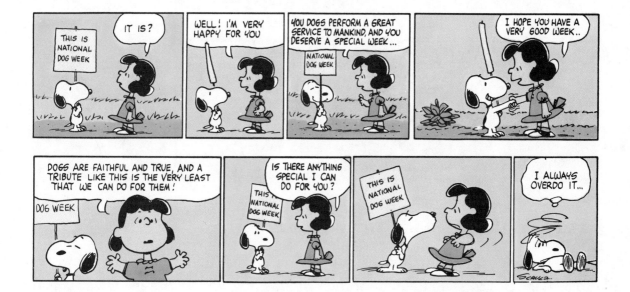

Why does a dog wag its tail?

Tail wagging is one of the ways that a dog "talks." You know that a dog is feeling happy when it wags its tail at you. Dogs also use tail wags to give special messages to other dogs. One kind of wag means, "Hello. Glad to see you." Another means, "I'm the boss around here." And a third means "Okay, you're the boss."

Why do dogs pant?

Dogs pant to cool off when they are feeling hot. People cool off by sweating, but dogs don't sweat very much. Instead, they breathe hard, with their tongues hanging out. This brings air into their bodies. The air cools their insides.

Why do dogs turn in circles before they lie down?

The ancestors of dogs were wild animals that lived outside. They turned around and around in circles to flatten grass and make a comfortable bed. Modern house dogs are still born with the instinct to make beds for themselves in this way —even though they no longer need this instinct. But wild dogs do need it. They still make their beds in grass by turning in circles.

Why do dogs gobble their food?

Charlie Brown is absolutely right. When dogs were wild, they didn't have owners to feed them. They had to hunt for their food. They would hunt in groups called packs. After they had killed an animal, each dog would try to get as much of the food as it could. But the wild dogs were not just trying to beat each other. If they didn't eat the food quickly, a larger animal might come along and take it away. Dogs today are still born with the instinct to gobble.

Earth's first space traveler was a dog!

Red Wolves

Do wolves ever attack people?

The wolves in the United States and Canada don't attack people. In fact, they stay as far away from people as possible. All the stories of wolf attacks probably grew up around Russian wolves. These wolves seem to be a more dangerous kind than the others. Even so, scientists don't believe most of the stories.

Why does a cow keep chewing when she isn't eating?

A cow has a special stomach with four parts. When she eats some grass, she chews it just enough to make it wet. Then it goes into the first part of her stomach, where it becomes softer. From there it goes into the second part, where it is made into little balls called "cuds." Later, while the cow is resting, she brings up each cud one at a time and chews it well. When she swallows it, the food goes into the third part of her stomach. There the water is squeezed out of it. Finally, the food goes to the fourth part of the cow's stomach and is broken down into very tiny pieces. Then the cow's body can take what it needs from the food to live and grow.

Do bulls really attack when they see red?

No, they don't. Bull fighters always wave a red cape in front of a bull. But the color red is not what makes the bull charge. In fact, the bull is color-blind. He cannot see the color red. Instead, the bull sees the movements of the cape and gets excited.

Bactrian Camel

Arabian Camel
or Dromedary

Why do camels have humps?

Camels live in the desert. They sometimes have to go for a long time without any food. That's when their humps become useful. The humps are made of fat. The camel can get its energy from the fat if it has no food. When the camel has not eaten for a few days, its humps get smaller. They get big again after the camel has filled itself up with food.

Is a pony a baby horse?

No, a baby horse is called a foal. A pony is a kind of horse that just happens to be small. When fully grown, it is between 32 and 58 inches tall. It weighs less than 800 pounds. That doesn't seem very small until you compare a pony to other horses. A large workhorse can weigh more than 2,000 pounds!

Shetland Pony

Workhorse

Why does a zebra have stripes?

A zebra's stripes help this animal to hide from enemies. When you see a zebra in the zoo, its stripes make it stand out clearly. But normally the zebra lives in places where there is very tall grass. There, the zebra's stripes blend in with the shadows of the blades of grass.

I'LL CALL IT ZEBRA SUNSET.

Which mammal is most like a human?

The chimpanzee. It is built a lot like us. It often walks on two feet the way we do. And, like us, it has no tail. However, the chimp is much smaller than a person. It has longer arms, shorter legs and a more hairy body.

The chimpanzee is probably the smartest animal next to man. A chimp can be taught to do almost everything a three-year-old child can do. One chimpanzee learned to say and understand a few English words. Others have learned to use the sign language of deaf and of mute people. Chimps have their own language, too. They have at least 20 different sounds that they use to "talk" to each other. Like humans, chimps show many different emotions in their faces. Sadly for the chimps, they also get human diseases such as cancer and tuberculosis.

What good is the giraffe's long neck?

With its long neck and long legs, the giraffe is the tallest animal in the world. Its head may be 19 feet above the ground. The giraffe's great height helps it in two ways. First, the giraffe can easily see a great distance over the flat open land where it lives. If a hungry lion is anywhere near, the giraffe will spot it soon enough to run away. Second, the giraffe can eat the leaves high up on trees. Other animals cannot reach these leaves. So the giraffe doesn't have to worry about their eating its food.

How does an elephant use its trunk?

A trunk is used as a nose, hand, and arm by an elephant. The elephant uses its trunk to smell, to feel along the ground, and to pick up objects. At the tip of its trunk it has either one or two "fingers" which can pick up something as small as a peanut. With its whole trunk, it can lift something as large as a tree.

An elephant uses its trunk to show affection. A mother pets her baby with her trunk. Both males and females pet each other with their trunks during mating season.

An elephant can also take up water with its trunk. It drinks by spraying the water into its mouth. Sometimes it sprays water all over its back. This shower keeps the elephant cool and clean.

141

Why does a kangaroo have a pouch?

A female kangaroo has a pouch so that her baby will have a place to live. When the kangaroo is born, it is only about an inch long — skinny, hairless, and very helpless. It is not yet ready to live in the outside world. So it crawls across its mother's body and into her pouch. There it can keep warm and safe and drink its mother's milk.

The baby kangaroo stays completely inside its mother's pouch about six months. Then it begins to stick its head out to eat leaves from low branches. When the baby kangaroo gets big enough to walk around, its mother still keeps an eye on it. She pulls it back into the pouch when danger is near.

WALTZING MATILDA

MELBOURNE

If you annoy a llama, it will spit in your face!

Spiny Anteater

Do any mammals lay eggs?

Yes, two kinds of mammals lay eggs. One is the platypus (PLAT-ih-pus), or duckbill, and the other is the spiny anteater. They are both called mammals because they have some kind of hair and the mothers feed their babies milk.

The female platypus lays from one to three eggs inside a hole in the ground. She keeps them warm with her tail until they hatch. Then she feeds the babies milk that comes out of the skin on her belly. Her way of feeding milk is different from that of most female mammals, whose milk comes out of special nipples on the chest or belly.

The female spiny anteater lays only one egg. She keeps it in a pouch that is something like a kangaroo's pouch. After it hatches, the baby stays in the pouch to drink milk that—like the platypus's milk—comes out of its mother's skin.

Platypus

Mastiff Bat

Pipistrelle Bat

Do any mammals fly?

Only one kind of mammal can fly—and that is the bat. Like birds, bats have wings that they can flap.

"Flying" squirrels and "flying" lemurs can't really fly—they glide. Instead of wings, these mammals have a piece of furry skin stretched between each front and back leg. This skin acts as a parachute when the animals leap from tree to tree.

Vampire

Natterer's Bat

How blind are bats?

Bats are not at all blind. They can see. In fact, some see very well. However, bats come out mostly at night and many of them have a hard time seeing in the dark. At night, these bats use their ears in place of eyes. The bats give out little clicking sounds. They can tell by the echo from each sound how near or far away an object is.

Mexican
Freetailed Bat

Hoary Bat

Most bats sleep hanging upside down!

144

You can tell what kind of food a bird eats just by looking at its bill. Seed-eating birds usually have short, stubby beaks—just right for cracking open seeds. The woodpecker's larger bill makes it easy to bore into trees and dig out insects. The eagle is a meat eater and its hooked beak helps it tear its food into bite-sized pieces. And the pelican uses the large pouch under its beak like a fishing net for scooping up fish.

Woodpecker

Bald eagle

There are more than 1,000,000 species (kinds) of animals. Insects account for 800,000 species. All the rest of the animals make up the remaining 200,000 species.

People who study animals are called zoologists (zoe-AHL-uh-jists). Scientists who study certain types of animals have special names. Here are a few:

scientist	subject
entomologist (en-tuh-MAHL-uh-jist)	insects
herpetologist (her-pih-TAHL-uh-jist)	reptiles
ichthyologist (ik-thee-AHL-uh-jist)	fish
ornithologist (or-nih-THAHL-uh-jist)	birds

California condor

Some animals have disappeared from the earth; they are extinct. Many others are now in danger of dying out forever.

There are fewer than 200 asiatic lions in the wilds of India. Only about 50 California condors still fly in the western skies of the United States. There are many animals that are threatened by extinction—from the huge rhinoceros to the tiniest fish.

Many governments of the world, with the help of zoos and international wildlife organizations, are beginning to protect the endangered species in their countries.

If you study tracks in the ground or snow in your neighborhood, you might be able to find out what animals live there. It will take a little practice, but soon you'll be able to learn the differences between the tracks of a bird, squirrel, dog, cat, mouse, and rabbit. Skilled trackers can even tell the difference between the tracks of a black bear and a grizzly bear.